Energy Healing
for
First Timers

Published By
LRM Publishing Limited

Written By
Lukshmiera Ramachandran Makwana

Copyright © 2021 LRM Publishing Limited

All rights reserved. No part of this book may be reproduced, stored in a retrieval system or transmitted in any form or by any means, without the prior written permission of the copyright owner/s or the publisher, LRM Publishing Limited.

All images in this book have been reproduced with the knowledge and prior consent of the artists and photographers concerned and no responsibility is accepted by the producer, publisher or printer for any infringement of copyright or otherwise, arising from the contents of this book.

Whilst the author has made every effort to ensure that the contents of this book are accurate in every particular way, it is not intended to be regarded as a substitute for professional medical advice for treatment.

The reader is urged to give careful consideration to any difficulties which he or she is experiencing with their own health and to consult their General Practitioner if uncertain as to its cause or nature.

Neither the author nor the publisher can accept any legal responsibility for any health problem which results from the use of the healing practices and self-help methods described.

ISBN: 9798489704694

Contents

Part 1: Introduction................7
    How this book is organised 8
    Preface 11

Part 2: Energy Healing 15
    Why do we need Energy Healing? 16
    What is Energy Healing? 18
    How does Energy Healing work? 20
    What are the Expectations, Risks and Recommendations of Energy Healing? .. 21

Part 3: Senses and Energy Healing 25
    What is meant by our Senses? 26
    How to use our Senses in Energy Healing 31

Part 4: Energy Healing Practices......... 33
    What are the seven Energy Healing practices? 34
    How to use the seven Energy Healing Practices to influence our Senses 35

    Energy Healing Practice 1
    Acupuncture 37
    How Acupuncture removes energy blockages.................. 38
    Frequently Asked Questions 39
    Self-care tips at home 42

Energy Healing Practice 2
Aromatherapy **47**

How Aromatherapy removes
energy blockages. 48

Frequently Asked Questions 49

Self-care tips at home 52

Energy Healing Practice 3
Chromotherapy **57**

How Chromotherapy removes
energy blockages. 58

Frequently Asked Questions 59

Self-care tips at home 62

Energy Healing Practice 4
Crystal Therapy. **67**

How Crystal Therapy removes
energy blockages. 68

Frequently Asked Questions 69

Self-care tips at home 72

Energy Healing Practice 5
Reflexology **77**

How Reflexology removes
energy blockages. 78

Frequently Asked Questions 79

Self-care tips at home 82

Energy Healing Practice 6
Reiki 87

How Reiki removes
energy blockages. 88

Frequently Asked Questions 89

Self-care tips at home 92

Energy Healing Practice 7
Sound Healing 99

How Sound Healing removes
energy blockages. 100

Frequently Asked Questions 101

Self-care tips at home 104

Part 5: Implementing in Practice 109

The Two Stage Approach 110

Reference Table 1
Body and Heart areas affected by Sense .114

Reference Table 2
Mind and Spirit areas affected by Sense .115

Readers' Notes 116

Part 6: Conclusion. 119

Conclusion 120

Acknowledgements 122

About the Author 123

Part 1:
Introduction

How this book is organised

This book provides an overview of energy healing for those considering it for the first time.

In this section, you will discover how this book has been organised into six parts. A summary of the content to be found in each part is provided below.

Part 1 – Introduction

This part provides a summary of how the book is organised and an insight into what inspired me to create this book.

Part 2 – Energy Healing

Part 2 explains how energy healing can help us, what energy healing is, how it works and the expectations, risks and recommendations of energy healing.

Part 3 – Energy Healing and Senses

Part 3 explains what is meant by our senses and how our senses can be used to receive energy healing.

Part 4 – Seven Energy Healing Practices

Part 4 commences with an introduction of what the seven energy healing practices are, the reasons for choosing to write about them and how they can be used to influence different senses in our bodies.

Each energy healing practice also features **three sections**:

1. **How it can remove energy blockages**
2. **The answers to these ten frequently asked questions:**
   1. What is the treatment?
   2. What objects are used in the treatment?
   3. Can anyone have this treatment?
   4. Do I need to undress for the treatment?
   5. What happens in a treatment session?
   6. How long will a treatment last?
   7. What does the treatment feel like?
   8. How many treatments will I need?
   9. What risks are associated with this treatment?
   10. Which health conditions is this energy healing practice most suitable for?
3. **Seven practical tips for self-care at home**

   The suggestions for self-care at home enable you to start healing straight away rather than having to wait to attend a treatment session in person.

Part 5 – Implementing in practice

Part 5 features an interactive two stage approach to help you to begin your healing journey and put all the learning gained from this book into practice.

The approach begins by identifying the pain/discomfort in the body so that the correct energy healing treatment is selected and the required results are achieved.

Part 6 – Conclusion

Part 6 provides a conclusion to the book and summarises the main learnings to take away with you to start living a better quality life.

This section also contains information about me as an author as well as acknowledgements to thank those people who have supported me on my journey as an author to create this book.

Preface

By writing this book, I hope to inspire and encourage people to become healthier versions of themselves by using the power of energy healing.

I experienced my first ever energy healing treatment about twenty years ago when I was in my teens. Then, energy healing was a new concept for me about which I knew very little. I therefore had no idea what to expect when I attended my first healing session but I remained open minded.

Prior to attending my first session, I tried to gather as much information as possible about energy healing. However, there was so much content available on the internet that it was difficult to know where to start. I felt overwhelmed and found myself becoming lost in the detail without getting the answers to what I wanted to know. So, I decided to simply proceed with the session and address the relevant questions and my concerns directly to the practitioner.

This is where the inspiration for my book came from. I realised how useful it would have been for me to have had access to a book like this before my first session; a book that would simplify the meaning of energy healing and would allow me to understand what to expect as a first timer.

So, following my first energy healing treatment, I began to read about others, trying many of them for myself which drove my curiosity even further. I decided to learn and understand more about the subject as a whole by attending courses, completing qualifications, experiencing more healing treatments and conversing with other healing professionals.

In addition, I visited many Hindu temples in South India to broaden my knowledge. During my travels, I became fascinated by the positivity and sense of calm that one feels on entering a Hindu temple. After leaving one of these temples, this happy and peaceful feeling would stay with me for sometimes up to a month afterwards.

I began to ponder what made me feel this way, as surely we would all want to feel this happiness in our lives all the time. After exploring this further, I understood that 'ENERGY' was the reason for this feeling.

I learned that during worship at Hindu temples, we can benefit from energy healing. Certain rituals that are performed can activate our five senses and help us to receive the energy we need.

1. **Smell** – by offering flowers to God at the temple.
2. **Taste** – by drinking holy water, known as "theertham".
3. **Sight** – by lighting camphor in front of the idol.
4. **Touch** – by putting hands over the camphor flames and then touching the eyes.
5. **Hearing** – by ringing the temple bell on entering the temple.

It was thanks to all these experiences that I began to truly appreciate the significance of energy and energy healing.

Energy healing changed my life for the better and I truly hope it does the same for you.

So, I invite you to continue reading to learn how energy healing can transform your life.

Part 2:
Energy Healing

Why do we need Energy Healing?

We all need energy healing to have a better quality of life. Energy healing encourages us to enjoy a happier and fuller existence.

Healing is a very individual process and therefore the definition of healing varies from person to person depending on their life circumstances. As such, for the purposes of this book, by healing I mean creating positive changes to our overall health and wellbeing.

Energy healing can help us to cope and move forward when we encounter difficulties in our lives.

The global pandemic experienced in 2019 has caused many people to suffer unexpected hardships in all aspects of their lives including health, love, relationships, money and careers.

As we face the difficulties that arise, we tend to put our bodies under a great deal of stress so that we are able to cope and get through the issues facing us.

This causes us to live in a constant state of stress. In small doses, stress can help us to accomplish tasks and prevent us from getting hurt. However, we are not designed to cope with stress on a long term basis.

Over time, stress becomes out of control, unmanaged and begins to compromise our health and wellbeing. Eventually, that stress manifests into physical ailments and discomfort or illness in the body such as neck and back pain.

Our initial thoughts when we become ill are to get rid of the problem as quickly as possible with a short term fix. We often succumb to taking medication as an immediate solution to pain relief and do not always allow ourselves to take the appropriate time to heal. As a consequence, we often find ourselves suffering from the same ailments again a few years later.

By focusing on treating specific health symptoms, we tend to overlook the underlying root causes of the ailments. By ignoring the underlying causes, our ailments will continue to fester until we address them.

Our physical ailments are not necessarily due to issues in the physical body alone. In our bodies, our hearts and minds are interdependent and vice versa.

This means that the cause of ailments may be a result of lingering negative emotions and thoughts that remain unresolved.

This is where energy healing can help by looking at the whole picture.

Energy healing focuses firstly on relieving the physical ailments in the body. Once this has been accomplished, it begins to establish the underlying issues that have caused the ailments. By recognising and healing these underlying causes, our health and wellbeing can be restored to their full potential.

What is Energy Healing?

We all are made of energy and we depend on a regular supply of it to stay alive. This is why we can heal using energy.

This energy is often referred to as life force, prana or chi and is thought to be the pure omnipresent energy that exists in every living being throughout the universe.

Energy healing uses our body's natural energy to bring about healing. This is achieved by directing energy to where it is most needed in the body and thereby returning it to its natural balance.

Everything in the universe is constantly moving, including our energy. The way in which energy moves is referred to as vibration. Energy frequency (measured in hertz (Hz) units) is the speed at which vibrations occur.

Every day we take part in an energy exchange to interact with other entities in the universe, such as nature and the people in our surroundings.

This means we can operate at high and low frequencies depending on our interactions and this can cause the amount and flow of energy within us to fluctuate daily.

When we are healthy, our energy flows abundantly and smoothly through us. However, when we encounter stress and difficulties in life, our energy can become stifled and can create energy blockages within us.

Energy blockages tend to reduce the amount of energy and how smoothly this energy flows. Eventually, these energy blockages result in physical ailments or illness in our bodies.

We can usually tell when we need a boost in our own energy levels, as we often experience the accompanying symptoms such as fatigue.

This is the time to turn to energy healing for support. Energy healing can remove these blockages, thereby returning our energy flow and balance as well as our health and wellbeing to their optimum levels.

How does Energy Healing work?

We all have the ability to improve our energy levels. Energy healing gives us the opportunity to raise our energy frequency through entrainment.

Entrainment occurs when two vibrating things such as objects or bodies lock into phase so that they can vibrate in harmony.

In most cases, when a person operating at a lower energy frequency comes into contact with a person, object or body point within an energy healing practice that is operating at a higher energy frequency, the lower energy frequency person will adjust and increase their energy frequency to synchronise with the higher energy frequency.

This higher energy frequency is directed towards the energy blockages in the body. The increased frequency level breaks apart the energy blockage and replenishes our energy so that we can heal.

What are the Expectations, Risks and Recommendations of Energy Healing?

Expectations

Every individual experiences energy healing differently depending on their own needs at the time.

During an energy healing treatment, it is usual for the recipient to expect a feeling of deep relaxation. Our nervous system, respiratory system, heart and brain are constantly working and require energy to function. Energy healing slows down these body parts and enables our energy to be free to move to the areas where it is needed. It is when our bodies are relaxed that our energy can entrain with other higher frequencies around us.

After the treatment, even though recipients tend to feel a little tired at first, they should usually expect to feel less pain, more energy and a general sense of wellbeing.

Energy healing is a cumulative process so, often, one treatment of an energy healing practice may not be sufficient to reach optimum health. The practitioner will advise how many sessions the recipient will need as each individual's healing needs are unique.

Precautions

Generally, energy healing is risk free and considered to be safe when carried out by a qualified professional who is professionally insured.

Although the energy healing practices featured in this book can be used by most people, it is always recommended that medical advice is sought from a GP regarding any health symptoms or pains the recipient is currently facing.

Pregnant women, epilepsy sufferers, those with pacemakers fitted, people with serious medical conditions and those with mental health problems should consult a medical practitioner prior to receiving energy healing treatments.

If an object or hand makes a recipient feel uncomfortable or unwell, for example, headaches or dizziness, then the recipient should inform the practitioner immediately so it can be removed.

Recommendations

It is recommended that plenty of time is allowed when booking the first visit. The initial appointment will be allocated a slightly longer time than subsequent visits to allow the practitioner to take a full medical history.

For the first appointment, it is advisable to take a list of medications and copies of any blood test results, x-rays or scans if relevant and to also wear comfortable clothing.

After an energy healing treatment session, it is a good idea to drink more water, avoid caffeine and alcohol, eat lighter meals and get more rest.

It is also recommended that, as the body may feel a little tired after a treatment, vigorous exercise is refrained from for the rest of that day but can be resumed the following day.

Part 3:
Senses and Energy Healing

What is meant by our Senses?

We all have senses in our bodies and we can receive energy healing by stimulating these senses. The behaviour of our senses can reveal whether energy blockages exist in our bodies. When there is a loss or distortion in our senses, this reveals that energy blockages are present.

Our senses are the main tools we use to understand more about ourselves, how our bodies are connected to each other and our universe and how to protect us from danger.

We have five key senses – smell, taste, sight, touch and hearing.

In addition to our five senses, energy healers believe that there are in fact two additional senses, the sixth being the sense of insight and the seventh being the sense of unity.

These two additional senses help us to achieve inner peace and spiritual enlightenment. They are eventually released once the energy balance in the other five senses has been restored.

Each of our senses resonates with specific areas of the body, emotions of the heart, thoughts of the mind and lessons of the spirit, the details of which can be found in the tables that follow.

Areas of the Body by Sense

Sense	Areas of the body that are affected
Smell	Hips, legs, lower back and male sexual organs
Taste	Kidneys, bladder, large intestine and female sexual organs
Sight	Stomach, liver, gall bladder, pancreas and small intestine
Touch	Heart, lungs, circulatory system, shoulders and upper back
Hearing	Throat, neck, teeth, ears and thyroid gland
Insight	Eyes, face, brain, lymphatic and endocrine systems
Unity	Central nervous system

Emotions of the Heart by Sense

Sense	Emotions of the heart that are affected
Smell	Anger, jealousy and aggression
Taste	Joy, feeling good or bad
Sight	Self-worth and confidence
Touch	Love and compassion
Hearing	Releasing feelings through expression
Insight	Permission to experience feelings
Unity	Cultivate bliss

Thoughts of the Mind by Sense

Sense	Thoughts of the mind that are affected
Smell	Stability, safety and survival
Taste	Pleasure and sociability
Sight	Determination, strength and personality
Touch	Acceptance and sincerity
Hearing	Communication, inspiration and expression
Insight	Intuition, trust and gratitude
Unity	Understanding, knowledge, spirituality

Lessons of the Spirit by Sense

Sense	Lessons of the spirit that are affected
Smell	Power of Freedom
Taste	Power of Choice
Sight	Power of Independence
Touch	Power of Love
Hearing	Power of Will
Insight	Power of Truth
Unity	Power of Divine Connection

How to use our Senses in Energy Healing

By stimulating our senses via energy healing we can remove the energy blockages relating to the physical body, emotions, thoughts and spiritual lessons.

On a physical level, energy healing triggers the body's natural healing abilities (immune system) by cleansing itself of toxins. As the toxins are removed, the body becomes re-generated.

On an emotional and mental level, energy healing aids the body in releasing stress and tension and clearing the mind of negative thoughts to improve decision making. Energy healing also helps to remove the negative emotion attached to a particular memory over time.

On a spiritual level, energy healing improves our intuition and spiritual guidance. Energy healing use tools that store and hold the universal life force energy. As such, energy healing helps us to deepen our connection with the universe and reinforce the truth that we are all one.

Part 4:
Energy Healing Practices

What are the seven Energy Healing practices?

There are seven energy healing practices described in this book:

These seven energy healing practices have been chosen because they are treatments that can be accomplished when a person visits a qualified practitioner. They are gentle, less invasive, work with our senses and can be combined together. For example, Crystal Therapy and Reiki would complement each other and thus the benefits of both could be gained from one treatment session.

The energy healing practices are therefore a realistic alternative to traditional methods of restoring health such as prescribed drugs, steroid injections or surgery and have the added benefit of being applied externally thereby avoiding any pressure or interference with any internal parts of the body.

How to use the seven Energy Healing Practices to influence our Senses

As mentioned previously, energy healing activates our senses. It is highly recommended that the energy healing practice that can influence a particular sense is tried in order to enhance healing.

For example, if you are experiencing pain in a particular area of the body, let us say the hips, this means that the smell sense corresponding to that area of the body has been disturbed.

The table, Areas of the Body by Sense, on page 27 provides detailed information about which areas of the body are affected by which sense.

Hence, you can use the energy healing practice, Aromatherapy, to stimulate the smell sense as demonstrated in the following table.

Sense	Energy Healing Practice
Smell	Aromatherapy
Taste	Aromatherapy
Sight	Chromotherapy, Crystal Therapy
Touch	Crystal Therapy, Acupuncture, Reflexology, Reiki
Hearing	Sound Healing
Insight	All
Unity	All

Energy Healing Practice 1
Acupuncture

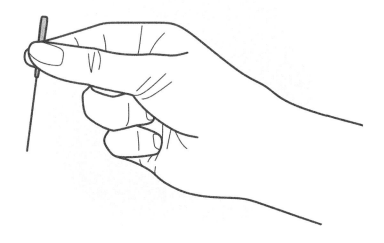

How Acupuncture removes energy blockages

Acupuncture points (or pressure points) have life force energy flowing through them.

When these points are stimulated, they can remove energy blockages in areas of the body because they have increased levels of energy frequency.

Acupuncture points respond well to needles due to their higher frequency. Needles are used to place pressure on an Acupuncture point to stimulate the nerve.

By stimulating the nerve, energy is produced that branches into the spine and is dispersed throughout the body. This process raises the vibrational level of the energy in and around the body.

Frequently Asked Questions

1. What is the treatment?

Acupuncture is a gentle, less invasive energy healing practice. It can be administered by needles into the different Acupuncture points of the body.

2. What objects are used during the treatment?

The needles that are inserted into different points of the body are fine and flexible disposable sterile needles (thickness of approximately 0.2mm). These needles are rounded at the tip so that they can be inserted smoothly into the skin.

Some practitioners also use indirect moxibustion, a traditional Chinese medicine technique that comprises the burning of mugwort (a small spongy herb) to promote healing. Indirect moxibustion involves lighting the end of a moxa stick and holding it close to the treatment area for a few minutes until the area turns red.

3. Can anyone have this treatment?

Yes, it is suitable for people of all ages and dispositions, including children and the elderly. However, the general precautions previously mentioned should still be considered.

4. Do I need to undress for the treatment?

The affected body parts will have to be exposed but usually there is no need to fully undress.

5. What happens during a treatment session?

At the start of the session, the acupuncturist may feel the recipient's pulse and then look at their tongue to gather information about their health. A healthy tongue is a pink colour, a swollen tongue indicates an allergy or infection and a smoother than normal tongue indicates nutrient deficiency.

The location of where the Acupuncture needle is inserted in the skin will depend on what condition the recipient is seeking to alleviate.

Having established this, the acupuncturist will then insert one or more thin needles into the skin or deeper so they reach the muscle of the recipient. Most practitioners will normally use between six to eight needles in a typical treatment.

The needles are kept in place from fifteen to thirty minutes.

6. How long will a treatment last?

A treatment session can last from twenty minutes to one hour, depending on the recipient's needs.

7. What does the treatment feel like?

Usually the recipient will feel very calm and relaxed. As each needle is inserted, the recipient is likely to feel only a mild, dull ache or a slight tingling sensation. Many Acupuncture needles come with a plastic guide tube that allows needles to be accurately inserted extremely quickly so that most people feel nothing at all.

8. How many treatments will I need?

One session may be sufficient, but it is more usual that eight to twelve sessions are needed.

9. What risks are associated with this treatment?

Acupuncture is dangerous if the recipient has a blood thinning disorder or circulation problems and thus Acupuncture is not advisable.

10. Which health conditions is this energy healing practice most suitable for?

Acupuncture can be used to treat many health problems such as stress, anxiety, depression, headaches, neck and back pain, arthritis, digestive problems, fertility and pregnancy related issues.

Nowadays, it is also used to rejuvenate the face because it helps to reduce the appearance of fine lines and wrinkles whilst also improving skin tone and colour.

Self-care tips at home

There are many ways that Acupuncture points can be incorporated into your daily life at home.

Due to the adverse risks (such as collapsed lungs) if the needles are inserted into the body incorrectly, Acupuncture is not recommended to be performed on yourself.

Therefore, I have set out alternative methods to Acupuncture which use fingertips instead of needles to apply pressure to the Acupuncture points in the body.

When we are stressed, these pressure points become blocked and restrict energy flow.

Healing can be achieved by using the relevant Acupuncture points as the same points are targeted in these treatments as well.

Acupressure (using hands)

The following three points can be stimulating using your thumb and fingers to reduce stress and anxiety. The union valley point and shoulder point can also help to alleviate headaches, muscle tension and neck pain.

UNION VALLEY

This point is located in the webbing between your thumb and index finger. Apply firm pressure using your index finger and thumb to the thumb and index finger of the other hand. Massage for four to five seconds.

SHOULDER POINT

This point can be found by pinching your shoulder muscle with your middle finger and thumb. Apply pressure and massage for five seconds.

FOREHEAD

This point is located at the midpoint between your eyebrows. Apply gentle pressure in a circular motion using your right thumb or forefinger for five to ten minutes.

Acupressure (using objects)

Small objects, for example, Spiky Balls which are readily available on Amazon, can be used to apply pressure instead of the fingertips. Spiky Balls are generally available in three different sizes with the smallest (3-5 cm) being suitable for smaller body parts such as the foot. The medium (8 cm) and large (10 cm) sizes are used for larger body parts such as the shoulder or gluteal whereby you can sit or lie on the Spiky Ball for one to two minutes and use your body weight to apply pressure to a tight muscle to encourage the muscles to relax.

SHOULDER

Standing with your Spiky Ball between your upper back muscles and a wall, use your body weight to roll over the ball applying pressure to any areas which feel tight.

GLUTEAL

Lie on your back with your knees bent and feet flat on the ground. Place your Spiky Ball underneath your buttocks and gently roll over the ball until you find a trigger point.

FOOT

Place the Spiky Ball underneath your foot and apply your body weight through the foot to roll the ball from your heel towards your toes.

Emotional Freedom Technique (EFT)

You can use the Emotional Freedom Technique (EFT) to address stress and anxiety issues. This technique targets nine points. For the best results it is advisable to tap each point and repeat the sequence seven times.

Begin by finger tapping (using your pointer and middle fingers of the dominant hand) the karate chop point then move down the body in the following order and finish the sequence at the top of the head.

1. KARATE CHOP – Between the top of the wrist and the side of the little finger
2. TOP OF THE HEAD – On the top of the head on the crown
3. EYEBROW – At the beginning of the eyebrow and above the nose
4. SIDE OF THE EYE – On the bone bordering the outside corner of the eye
5. UNDER THE EYE – On the bone under the centre of one eye

6. UNDER THE NOSE – In the space between your nose and upper lip
7. CHIN – In the indent below your lips and above your chin
8. BEGINNING OF THE COLLARBONE – At the junction where the sternum (breastbone), collarbone and the first rib meet
9. UNDER THE ARM – One inch below the armpit

Energy Healing Practice 2
Aromatherapy

How Aromatherapy removes energy blockages

Essential oils use the pure energy of plants to remove energy blockages in areas of the body because essential oils have an increased level of energy frequency.

When essential oils are inhaled, they stimulate our smell receptors which send electrical impulses to the brain. When they are applied to the body during a massage, the oils enter the skin through the hair follicles where they are absorbed into the blood stream and circulate around the body. Both these processes raise the vibrational level of the energy in and around the body.

Frequently Asked Questions

1. What is the treatment?

Aromatherapy (or Essential Oil Therapy) is a gentle non-invasive energy healing practice. It utilises essential oils by breathing their aroma in through the nose or by putting the oils on the skin.

2. What objects are used during the treatment?

The common essential oils used in Aromatherapy are lavender for inhalation and lavender, peppermint, bergamot, rose or geranium for massage. The oils are diluted with a carrier oil, such as sweet almond or grapeseed, due to their concentrated nature.

Some practitioners may also burn scented candles in the treatment room so that the recipient can benefit from essential oils by inhaling them. The most common scents are lavender and lemon. Lavender can relieve tension and is ideal to aid relaxation. Citrus scents can release stress and enhance overall mood.

3. Can anyone have this treatment?

Yes, it is suitable for people of all ages and dispositions, including children and the elderly although the general precautions previously mentioned should still be considered.

However, care should be taken when treating children and the elderly. Children's skin is more sensitive so the essential oils used should be half the strength of that used for adults. The elderly may suffer from allergies, chronic pain and poor skin which prevents the use of essential oils and massage. There are some instances where the oils may interfere with prescribed medication.

4. Do I need to undress for the treatment?

Usually, for a full treatment Aromatherapy massage, the recipient will need to fully undress.

5. What happens during a treatment session?

At the start of the session, the practitioner will prepare and combine a blend of oils selected by the recipient.

The essential oils that are mixed and used will depend on the condition they are seeking to alleviate and how the recipient wants to feel, for instance, rose oil for uplifting or eucalyptus oil for decongesting. The session usually begins with three deep inhalations of the oil or oils that the recipient has chosen.

A full body massage usually begins with the back, bottom and legs before the recipient turns over and the practitioner massages the front part of the body including the head and stomach.

The practitioner glides over the recipient's skin with the hands using the essential oil or oils and combines this with deeply soothing massage techniques such as long sweeping strokes and deep kneading action. For the face, the practitioner will use soothing strokes with the fingertips on the temples and forehead.

6. How long will a treatment last?

A treatment session can last from thirty minutes to an hour and a half, depending on the recipient's needs.

7. What does the treatment feel like?

Usually the recipient will feel very calm and relaxed. An Aromatherapy massage should be gentle and firm and not intense. However, different practitioners apply a different amount of pressure to help release muscle tension. It is therefore advisable to advise the practitioner at the start of the treatment what type of pressure is preferred, for instance, light/mild, medium or hard.

8. How many treatments will I need?

One session may be sufficient, but it is more usual that eight to ten sessions will be required.

9. What risks are associated with this treatment?

Essential oils used in Aromatherapy may cause an allergic skin reaction and those with sensitive skin, scars or burns or who are sensitive to scents are advised not to have Aromatherapy treatment. If citrus oils are used then the recipient should avoid exposure to the sun for twelve to eighteen hours following the treatment.

10. Which health conditions is this energy healing practice most suitable for?

Aromatherapy can be used to treat many health problems such as stress, anxiety, depression, headaches, nausea, long lasting pain and skin issues.

Nowadays, the essential oil, eucalyptus, is used in steam inhalations to treat upper respiratory problems by fighting infection and opening air passages making it easier to breathe.

Self-care tips at home

There are many ways that essential oils can be incorporated into your daily life at home.

However, due to the concentrated nature of essential oils, gloves should be worn when handling these.

When we become stressed, the muscles close to our skin tend to contract. This can leave our skin undernourished with blood making it look much drier than normal skin. When the muscles are tense, they can cause us to ache. We can also feel fatigued and encounter digestive issues.

Healing can be achieved by using the relevant essential oils.

Muscular Aches

COMPRESS

Hot compresses using essential oils can help to relieve muscular aches such as backache, menstrual pain and arthritic pain.

A compress can be made by adding two drops of both rosemary and marjoram essential oils into a bowl of hot water and soaking a face cloth in this before applying to the affected area.

FOOT BATH

Soak your feet in a mini bath by adding five to ten drops of essential oil to a large basin two thirds full of hot water. The warmth of the water helps circulation to improve and soothes aches and pains. Peppermint essential oil is the ideal oil for using in a refreshing foot bath. For hot aching feet, add two drops of peppermint and two drops of lemon oil.

Digestion

Herbal teas are composed of essential oils and can be used to help with digestive issues such as indigestion and bloating. Lemon and ginger, peppermint and chamomile teas are commonly used to calm the stomach by placing the tea leaves or bags in a mug of hot water and drinking this.

Sore Throat

Gargling two drops of antiseptic essential oil (such as tea tree) mixed in a quarter of a cup of salt water can help to relieve sore throats by interacting with the bacteria that is causing the infection.

Sleep

Sprinkle or spray a few drops of lavender essential oil onto your pillow before you go to bed to promote a better night's sleep. Alternatively, you can use a lavender room spray or a lavender sleep pillow which is filled with fragrant dried lavender.

Moisturiser

A simple moisturiser infused with essential oil can be used to revive your skin. Three drops of sandalwood and three drops of rose oil can be mixed into your favourite 25g pot of skin cream.

Revitalise

Essential oils such as rosemary or peppermint oil can give an instant uplift and make you feel more alert when you are feeling tired. Add one to two drops of these oils to a burner which involves adding the chosen oils to a bowl and then placing the bowl over a lighted tea light which will gently heat the oils. Alternatively, add three drops of rosemary and two drops of peppermint to a bowl of steaming water and allow the oils to evaporate into the room.

Energy Healing Practice 3
Chromotherapy

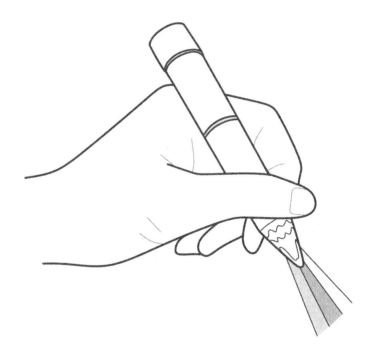

How Chromotherapy removes energy blockages

Colours use energy from light to remove energy blockages in areas of the body because colours have increased levels of energy frequency.

Colours are directly captured by the light receptor cells in the retina of the eyes and are converted into electrical impulses in the brain. This process raises the vibrational level of the energy in and around the body.

Frequently Asked Questions

1. What is the treatment?

Chromotherapy (or Colour Therapy) is a gentle non-invasive energy healing practice. It is administered by diverting coloured light onto different parts of the body.

2. What objects are used during the treatment?

A small spotlight onto which coloured glass filters are attached can be used in this treatment. Alternatives to a spotlight are a Chromotherapy torch or glass bottled liquids of different colours. This equipment is often utilised as it can be used to move around the recipient with ease.

3. Can anyone have this treatment?

Yes, it is suitable for people of all ages and dispositions, including children and the elderly. However, the general precautions previously mentioned should still be considered.

4. Do I need to undress for the treatment?

The recipient will usually remain fully clothed during this treatment.

5. What happens during a treatment session?

At the start of the session, the practitioner will prepare the coloured lights to be used based on the colours selected by the recipient. The recipient usually selects three colours from a range of coloured cards. The first colour represents the present situation. The second colour will indicate the area of challenge now facing them. The third colour can then be chosen to indicate what colour vibrations should be worked with to meet those challenges.

The colours used will depend on what condition they seeking to alleviate.

The practitioner then starts the session by shining green light on the upper part of the body and magenta light on the lower part of the body to restore an initial energy balance.

Concentrated coloured lights are then continued to be shone directly onto specific areas of the body. This treatment relies on a specific colour and its complementary colour being used. The complementary colour is the opposite colour from the one needed as featured on a standard eight colour wheel. For example, the complementary colour for red is blue.

6. How long will a treatment last?

A treatment session can last from forty minutes to an hour and a half, depending on the recipient's needs.

7. What does the treatment feel like?

Usually the recipient will feel very calm and relaxed. Some people feel sensations of heat, coolness, tingling, pulsing or mild pins and needles. Some may experience seeing colours and white light.

8. How many treatments will I need?

One session may prove sufficient but it is more usual for four to six sessions to be necessary.

9. What risks are associated with this treatment?

Coloured light used in Chromotherapy can have a detrimental effect on those who have sensitive sight, albinism and those who suffer from photosensitive epilepsy.

10. Which health conditions is this energy healing practice most suitable for?

Chromotherapy can be used to treat many health problems such as stress, anxiety, depression, nerve disorders, digestive problems, blood and circulation problems and fevers.

Nowadays, Chromotherapy is used in the form of phototherapy (blue coloured light) specifically administered to new born babies suffering from jaundice. Jaundice is a medical condition that causes yellowing of the skin.

Self-care tips at home

There are many ways that colours can be incorporated into your daily life at home.

When we become stressed, we tend to reject certain colours to reflect our mood as colours have a profound effect on our emotions. For example, to uplift mood use yellow and orange while for healing from illness use violet, indigo and blue.

Healing can be achieved by using the relevant colours.

Clothing

Coloured clothing can be worn and it is recommended that only natural fibres such as silk or cotton should be used to align with your energy.

Colours worn could include these rainbow colours:

1. SMELL – Red
2. TASTE – Orange
3. SIGHT – Yellow
4. TOUCH – Green
5. HEARING – Blue
6. INSIGHT – Indigo
7. UNITY – Violet

Seasonal colours can also be worn. Spring and autumn colours are warm such as green and coral while summer and winter colours tend to be cool such as blue and pink.

Food

Colour can be ingested using food that represents the rainbow colours.

1. RED – Strawberries, beetroot
2. ORANGE – Oranges, carrots
3. YELLOW – Bananas, yellow peppers
4. GREEN – Green apples, kale
5. BLUE – Blueberries, blue corn
6. INDIGO – Plums, purple grapes
7. VIOLET – Eggplant, passion fruit

For example, if you suffer from insomnia then eating light meals including blue and green foods will be beneficial.

Solarised Water

Colour can be ingested by solarising water. You must use only pure natural spring water and pour this into a coloured glass bottle. Place this in the sunlight for thirty to sixty minutes.

The water must be consumed the same day for maximum benefit. Blue water is a great healer, in particular for issues relating to the nose, throat, ears or eyes.

Flowers

Specific flowers can also be used to enhance healing by surrounding oneself with the colours.

1. RED – Red roses
2. ORANGE – Orange birds of paradise
3. YELLOW – Yellow dandelions
4. GREEN – Green orchids
5. BLUE – Blue bluebells
6. INDIGO – Purple hydrangea
7. VIOLET – White jasmine

Home Decor

Colours such as peaches and creams can be used to create a relaxed environment at home. These colours have muscle relaxant qualities that aid sleep.

Colouring Books/Applications

Colouring books with a mandala pattern can calm and relax the mind. There are many free applications that can be downloaded such as "Color by Numbers" that require colouring by following numbers to bring images to life.

Colour Breathing/Rainbow Meditation

Colour breathing uses the rainbow colours. Breathe in each colour three or four times while resting in between colours. Starting with red and inhaling each rainbow colour in turn until you reach violet. While focusing on the colour, slowly breathe out sending the colour throughout your body.

Energy Healing Practice 4
Crystal Therapy

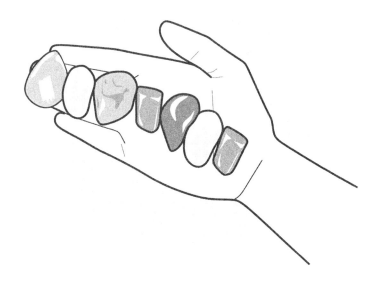

How Crystal Therapy removes energy blockages

Crystals resemble three dimensional lattices and use natural powerful energy to remove energy blockages in areas of the body because they hold an increased level of energy frequency.

When crystals are placed on the body, energy is conducted and amplified throughout the body due to the mineral content residing in the crystals. This process raises the vibrational level of the energy in and around the body.

Frequently Asked Questions

1. What is the treatment?

Crystal Therapy is a gentle non-invasive energy healing practice that can be administered through crystals, by holding or placing these on and around different parts of the body.

2. What objects are used during the treatment?

Some practitioners only use one or two crystals from the quartz family during a healing session since quartz crystals are able to hold and amplify energy. The common crystals used from the quartz family are clear quartz, rose quartz, amethyst and citrine.

Sometimes the practitioner will use a dowsing crystal pendulum to help to determine where the crystals should go. A pendulum is a crystal suspended on a chain that intuitively swings in one direction or the other in response to yes or no questions.

3. Can anyone have this treatment?

Yes, it is suitable for people of all ages and dispositions, including children and the elderly. However, the general precautions previously mentioned should still be considered.

4. Do I need to undress for the treatment?

The recipient will usually remain fully clothed during this treatment.

5. What happens during a treatment session?

Before the crystals can be used in the session, they will need to be cleansed and charged. Cleansing removes any negative energy the crystals have stored and charging brings positive energy into the crystals. Normally, crystals are cleansed in moonlight and charged in the sunlight.

The practitioner will place the specific crystals on the recipient's body or in their hands or any areas of the body either singly or in patterns (called grids).

On the body, rainbow coloured crystals are normally placed in seven particular areas with red being at the base of the spine, orange below the navel, yellow at the abdomen, green at the heart, blue at the throat, indigo in the middle point of the forehead and violet on the top of the head.

The crystals are kept in each position for five to fifteen minutes depending on how much healing the recipient needs at each position.

6. How long will a treatment last?

A treatment session can last from twenty minutes to an hour, depending on the recipient's needs.

7. What does the treatment feel like?

Usually, the recipient will feel very calm and relaxed. Some people feel sensations of heat, coolness, tingling or pulsing from the crystals on the areas where they have been placed on the body. Some may experience seeing colours, white light and feeling either heavy or a sense of weightlessness as though they are floating on air.

8. How many treatments will I need?

One session may be sufficient, but it is more usual that three or four sessions are necessary.

9. What risks are associated with this treatment?

There are no major risks associated with this treatment. However, special precautions need to be taken if the recipient has metal pins, plates or a pacemaker fitted.

10. Which health conditions is this energy healing practice most suitable for?

Crystal Therapy can be used to treat many health problems such as stress, anxiety, depression, insomnia, headaches, concentration and memory, muscle aches and pains, blood and circulation problems and arthritis.

Epsom salts can be used in the bath to ease muscle inflammation, help circulation and soothe aches and pains. The salts contain the mineral magnesium which has healing properties and can be absorbed through the skin. They are composed primarily of sodium chloride which has a crystalline structure, hence their effectiveness in Crystal Therapy.

Self-care tips at home

There are many ways that crystals can be incorporated into your daily life at home.

When we become stressed, we tend to reject certain crystals depending on their colours and properties if these fail to align with the emotions that we feel at a specific moment in time.

Healing can be achieved by using the relevant crystals.

Wearing Crystals

Crystals can be worn on the body as a bracelet, necklace or pendant.

It is worth noting that the healing may take some time when the crystal is worn as it is only in contact with one small area of the body. If you find wearing crystals uncomfortable then you can keep a crystal in your purse or near your bed.

The appropriate crystals to be worn can include the rainbow colours.

1. SMELL – Red jasper
2. TASTE – Carnelian
3. SIGHT – Citrine
4. TOUCH – Aventurine
5. HEARING – Howlite
6. INSIGHT – Amethyst
7. UNITY – Clear quartz

Meditate

Meditate by focusing your attention on your breathing while holding crystals, rose quartz or amethyst. Rose quartz is used to introduce love to all relationships and amethyst is an all-encompassing healing stone. Breathe in deeply through your nose and out through your mouth, noticing as the air moves in and out your body.

You can also meditate using malas (strands) of 108 beads made of coloured crystals with a 'guru' head bead to indicate where to begin and end. 108 represents the universe as being one, empty and infinite.

Hold your mala in your right hand, draped between your middle and index fingers. You can recite a mantra 108 times aloud or silently while working your way around the mala. (Refer to the Self-care tips at home in the Sound Healing section for mantra options).

Bath Salts

Himalayan salts can be used in a body bath to detox the body and release negative energy into the bath water. Fill your bath with five inches of water and then add two to four salt rocks to the bath. Stir the water until the salt is mostly dissolved. Submerge your body in the bath for around twenty to thirty minutes.

Face Products

Crystals are used in beauty products where they are finely ground and mixed into the product to help exfoliate and illuminate the skin. Rose quartz can be found in face polish and tourmaline in face masks.

Technology Devices

Crystals can be used to protect you from the negativity obtained from your mobile phone, tablet and laptop. Place black tourmaline on top of these devices for five to ten minutes.

Cars

Crystals can be placed in your car to protect you from negativity when driving. Black tourmaline is often used as it can strongly absorb negative energy and is usually placed on the dashboard or in the glove compartment of the car.

Indoor Potted Plants

You can use the crystals clear quartz or green aventurine to help the plants to heal and grow. Gently push the chosen crystal into the soil.

Energy Healing Practice 5
Reflexology

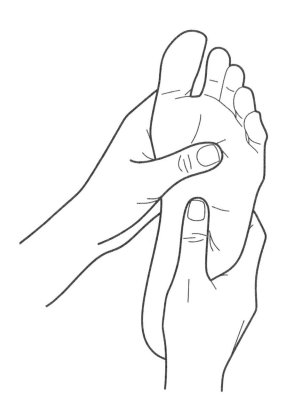

How Reflexology removes energy blockages

Reflexology points, or pressure points, have life force energy flowing through them.

These points can remove energy blockages in areas of the body when they are stimulated because Reflexology points have increased levels of energy frequency and therefore respond well to touch. Fingers and thumbs are used to place pressure on Reflexology points to stimulate the nerve.

By stimulating the nerve, the energy that is produced branches into the spine and is dispersed throughout the body. This process raises the vibrational level of the energy in and around the body.

Frequently Asked Questions

1. What is the treatment?

Reflexology is a gentle non-invasive energy healing practice that can be administered by touching different pressure points or Reflexology points on the feet, lower leg, hands, face or ears. Reflexology (reflex) points are areas of the body that reflex back to specific parts of the body.

2. What objects are used during the treatment?

Practitioners apply pressure with the hands by "thumb walking" whereby the thumb (or finger) bends and straightens whilst maintaining a constant pressure across the feet, lower leg, hands, ears or face depending on the type of Reflexology chosen. Sometimes the treatment can also incorporate the knuckles and small wooden sticks.

3. Can anyone have this treatment?

Yes, it is suitable for people of all ages and dispositions, including children and the elderly. However, the general precautions previously mentioned should still be considered.

4. Do I need to undress for the treatment?

The feet will have to be exposed so the recipient will be requested to remove just their shoes and socks for treatment to take place.

5. What happens during a treatment session?

In foot Reflexology, the toes and feet indicate the head and neck. The insides of the feet correlate to the spine and the area just underneath the toes corresponds to the chest. The thinnest part of the foot, usually found towards its centre, is known as the waistline. The parts of the foot correlated with the stomach are found above the waistline. The parts correlated with the intestines are found below. Finally, the bottom of the foot is connected with the pelvic area.

The practitioner may start the session by washing the recipient's feet and soaking them in warm water and then position the feet at his or her chest level while the recipient sits or lies down.

The practitioner will apply pressure directly to the required Reflexology points, using one finger or thumb to push down in a gentle circular motion clockwise for about six rotations and then anti-clockwise for another six rotations.

6. How long will a treatment last?

A treatment session can last from thirty minutes to an hour and a half, depending on the recipient's needs.

7. What does the treatment feel like?

Usually the recipient will feel very calm and relaxed. Most people feel a sense of lightness, tingling and feelings of warmth. If reflexologists find pain, congestion or tightness during the session, they will apply pressure to release this. However, different practitioners apply different amounts of pressure to help release muscle tension. For this reason, it is best to inform the practitioner at the beginning of the treatment what type of pressure is preferred, for instance, light/mild, medium or hard.

8. How many treatments will I need?

One session may be sufficient, but it is more usual that one session a week for six weeks is needed.

9. What risks are associated with this treatment?

Reflexology is dangerous if the recipient has a blood thinning disorder or circulation problems. Special precautions should be taken for a recipient with foot fractures, unhealed wounds or active gout. Recipients fitting into these categories are advised not to have Reflexology.

10. Which health conditions is this energy healing practice most suitable for?

Reflexology can be used to treat many health problems such as stress, anxiety, nasal congestion, eyesight, lung conditions such as asthma, nerve disorders, digestive problems, kidney function, diabetes, blood and circulation problems and memory as well as relieving discomfort from menstruation.

A knee jerk reflex diagnostic tool is used to diagnose and treat conditions that affect the nervous system. The knee jerk reflex is when the doctor taps the patient's knee with a hammer and the result is that the knee kicks out.

Self-care tips at home

There are many ways that Reflexology points can be incorporated into your daily life at home.

When we are stressed, these pressure points become blocked and restrict energy flow.

Healing can be achieved by using the relevant Reflexology points in the feet, hands and face.

Feet

HEADACHES

The big toe can relieve headaches and neck pain. Start by using your fingers to create circular rubbing movements on your big toes. Next apply more pressure to the upper halves of each toe. Massage each toe for sixty seconds.

BREAST POINT

It is often thought that we hold negative emotions in our chest area. To release these emotions, we can press the breast reflex point (rectangle area) on the top of the foot. This area extends from the base of your toes to slightly below your big toe knuckle.

Using the knuckles with the hand held in a fist, firmly press up and down this area for thirty to sixty seconds in both feet simultaneously.

BACK PAIN

The spinal Reflexology points are located on the bottom half of the soles of your feet. Rub these areas for two minutes.

Hands

PAIN

Each step should be stimulated for a minute on each hand simultaneously.

1. Rub your thumb in wide movements over the palm, working out from the centre to the edges.
2. Gently rub down in long, straight motions from the knuckles to the wrist.
3. Wrap your hand round each finger one by one and gently rotate at the joint.
4. Stimulate the Reflexology points by pinching the end of each finger.
5. Starting at the base of each finger, rub in small anti-clockwise circles until you reach the tip.
6. Apply gentle pressure in small circles all over the palms and backs of the hand, working down to the wrist.

Mudras (hand gestures)

Mudras are ways to access your Reflexology points. Each mudra should be held for at least five minutes.

MEMORY

This mudra can be performed by touching your index fingertip to the tip of your thumb, while holding your other three fingers straight.

PEACE

This mudra can be performed by placing the outside of your right hand into the palm of your left hand with the tips of the thumbs touching and both palms facing upwards.

METABOLISM AND DIGESTION

This mudra can be performed by bending your ring finger to the base of your thumb so that your thumb touches the ring finger's knuckles. Try to stretch your other three fingers as straight as possible without stressing the hand.

Energy Healing Practice 6
Reiki

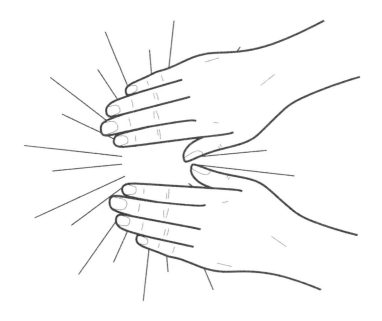

How Reiki removes energy blockages

Reiki uses divine energy to remove energy blockages in areas of the body because the divine energy has an increased level of energy frequency and can change the life force energy with its higher frequency.

Reiki (pronounced 'Ray Kee') is a Japanese word meaning 'universal life force energy'. Rei translates as 'spirit', meaning God, and Ki is the universal life force energy.

When Reiki is applied on the body using the hands, energy is passed from the practitioner to the recipient because the practitioner acts as a conduit to Reiki. This process raises the vibrational level of the energy in and around the body.

Frequently Asked Questions

1. What is the treatment?

Reiki is a gentle non-intrusive energy healing practice that can be administered by placing the hands lightly on different parts of the body.

2. What objects are used during the treatment?

Reiki is unique in the fact that the recipient can only use the technique if they have been attuned. A Reiki attunement is the process by which a person receives the healing ability of Reiki energetically from a Reiki Master during a Reiki class.

There are typically three levels of Reiki training (Level 1, Level 2 and Master Level). It is at Reiki Level 2 where students receive three symbols (power, harmony and connection) and at Master level where students receive the final two symbols (mastery and completion).

Once they have received the attunement, they can treat themselves (after successful completion of the Reiki 1 course) as well as others (after successful completion of the Reiki 2 course).

3. Can anyone have this treatment?

Yes, it is suitable for people of all ages and dispositions, including children and the elderly. However, the general precautions previously mentioned should still be considered.

4. Do I need to undress for the treatment?

The recipient will usually remain fully clothed during this treatment.

5. What happens during a treatment session?

Reiki practitioners often use Reiki symbols to connect and enhance Reiki power in the session. To activate the symbols, the practitioners can visualise them, say their names out loud or even draw them in the air with their hands. The practitioner can then use the Reiki symbols to set an intention for Reiki to work for the highest good of the recipient.

The practitioner gently places their hands in specific places on or near the body. Reiki practitioners tend to use twelve hand positions during a treatment (as detailed in the distant Reiki healing section) four on the head (top of the head, brow, temples/ears and throat), four on the front of the body (heart, solar plexus, navel and base of spine pelvic bone) and four on the back of the body (top of the shoulders, middle back, waist and bottom).

The hands are kept in each position for three to ten minutes depending how much Reiki the recipient needs at each position.

The practitioner ends the session with a clearing of the negative blockages with a sweeping movement starting at the head and brushing down to the toes.

6. How long will a treatment last?

A treatment session can last from forty-five minutes to an hour and a half, depending on the recipient's needs.

7. **What does the treatment feel like?**

   Usually the recipient will feel very calm and relaxed. Some people feel sensations of heat, coolness, tingling, pulsing or experience seeing colours. Some people often feel a sense of weightlessness.

8. **How many treatments will I need?**

   One session may be sufficient, but it is more usual that three or four sessions are necessary.

9. **What risks are associated with this treatment?**

   Reiki is generally considered a risk free energy healing practice. A temporary aggravation of symptoms can occur when people suffering from chronic conditions choose to receive multiple sessions in quick succession. Some recipients can experience a short term upset stomach, light headedness and fatigue following treatment.

10. **Which health conditions is this energy healing practice most suitable for?**

    Reiki can be used to treat many health problems such as stress, anxiety, depression, insomnia, infertility, autism, fatigue and chronic pain.

    Nowadays, Reiki is often used in palliative care as it helps to control the side effects of cancer treatments such as pain, anxiety and sickness.

Self-care tips at home

There are many ways that Reiki can be incorporated into your daily life.

When we are stressed, certain parts of our body become blocked and restrict energy flow.

Healing can be achieved by using the relevant hand positions.

Self-Treatment

EIGHT HAND POSITIONS

After completing Reiki Level 1, it is important to practice Reiki daily as a self-treatment to strengthen your Reiki connection. Self-treatment uses eight of the twelve hand positions previously mentioned in the answer to question 5. In addition to these hand positions, you may also place your hands on your back or legs if needed.

Set aside a regular time daily to perform self-treatment in a quiet space. You can play relaxing instrumental music or music specific to Reiki with a three minute bell to remember to change hand positions when the bell rings. It is suggested that you begin with a twenty minute treatment first thing in the morning before you start your day.

THREE POINTS

If you are short of time, you can self-treat using only three points on the body using the associated symbols as outlined below.

After connecting to Reiki, place your hands on the first point. Draw the symbol or say the mantra attached to the symbol three times. Hold your hands in each position for three minutes. After this, continue repeating the same method for the other points.

1. Hara: Located at the lower abdomen. Draw the Power symbol or say the mantra, "Cho Ku Rei."

2. Third Eye: Located at the middle of the forehead. Draw the Harmony symbol or say the mantra, "Sei HeKi."

3. Heart: Located at the heart. Draw the Connection symbol or say the mantra, "Hon Sha Ze Sho Nen."

Distant Healing

Distant healing can be used to give Reiki to others without the need for physical touch. This can be done because Reiki is not restricted by time or space. The healing session usually starts by drawing the connection symbol and setting an intention to join the practitioner and recipient together. After this, a full distant Reiki treatment (lasting thirty to forty-five minutes) can be received using the below twelve hand positions. At the end of the session, the practitioner can clap three times releasing the connection from the recipient.

1. TOP OF THE HEAD

   One hand is placed under the recipient's head and this hand forms a comfortable cradle for the head. The other hand is placed on the top of the head, the crown.

2. BROW

   Both hands are placed over the recipient's face, with the palms gently on the forehead and the fingers cupped lightly over the eyes.

3. TEMPLES/EARS

   The recipient's ears are surrounded around the jawline, with the palms touching the temples and fingers lightly on the ears.

4. THROAT

   The recipient's collarbone is surrounded by the palms of the practitioner in a U shape.

5. HEART

   Both hands are placed over the heart centre.

6. SOLAR PLEXUS

   Both hands are placed on the upper rib cage below the chest area.

7. NAVEL

    Both hands are placed on the abdomen above the recipient's navel.

8. BASE OF SPINE

    One hand is placed over each pelvic bone.

9. TOP OF THE SHOULDERS

    Both hands are placed on the shoulder blades.

10. MIDDLE BACK

    Both hands are placed on the middle back area

11. WAIST

    Continuing down the back of the body, both hands are placed on the recipient's lower back

12. BOTTOM

    The hands are placed slightly above this private area.

Other Uses

You can receive Reiki when you use Reiki on other living beings as you act as a conduit to Reiki.

ANIMALS

Reiki can be used on animals to help them to recover from illnesses, diseases and from past neglect.

PLANTS

Reiki can be used on plants to help them to recover, grow and become stronger.

WATER

Reiki can be used to charge a glass of drinking water. Drinking Reiki water can help to alleviate physical symptoms or medical side effects as it has the same effect as a Reiki treatment.

CLEANSING THE HOME

Reiki can be used in your home to alter the energy by cleansing and protecting you from negativity.

Energy Healing Practice 7
Sound Healing

How Sound Healing removes energy blockages

Sound Healing uses energy waves to remove energy blockages in areas of the body because sounds have increased levels of energy frequency.

When sound is heard through our ears, the cells in our body absorb and emit the sound to different parts of the body. This process raises the vibrational level of the energy in and around the body.

Frequently Asked Questions

1. What is the treatment?

Sound Healing is a gentle non-intrusive energy healing practice. It can be administered through sound by placing instruments on and around different parts of the body and playing them.

2. What objects are used during the treatment?

The Himalayan metal singing bowls are named thus because they sing "OM" which continues to sound for a long time after they have been played.

These bowls are made with alloys that usually contain from five to seven precious metals that are connected to the planets of our galaxy. The size of the bowl and the ratio between the metals affect the pitch, vibration and quality of the sound produced by the bowl.

3. Can anyone have this treatment?

Yes, it is suitable for people of all ages and dispositions, including children and the elderly. However, the general precautions previously mentioned should still be considered.

4. Do I need to undress for the treatment?

The recipient will usually remain fully clothed during this treatment.

5. What happens during a treatment session?

The practitioner places seven handmade metal bowls of different sizes and metals (a mixture of copper and tin) on or around the recipient in particular locations. The largest bowl is placed at the feet to encourage grounding and the smallest bowl is placed at the head.

The sounds used will depend on what condition they are seeking to alleviate.

The Himalayan singing bowls are struck with a mallet or wand. They, in turn, emit and produce a melodic tone representing a note of a musical scale. When the side of the mallet is rubbed against the rim or hit on the side of the singing bowl, the bowls sing on that same musical note.

Initially the practitioner will tap each bowl three times with a ten second interval between each tap.

This gap allows the sound to resonate and tune in to the recipient's body properly.

Throughout the session, the practitioner will continue to move around the recipient, circling and striking each bowl and occasionally hitting symbols against each other just above the head.

6. How long will a treatment last?

A singing bowls therapy session can last from thirty to forty-five minutes, depending on the recipient's needs.

7. What does the treatment feel like?

Usually the recipient will feel very calm and relaxed. Some people feel sensations of heat, coolness and tingling and experience seeing colours and feeling emotional. Some people often feel a sense of weightlessness as though they are floating on air.

8. How many treatments will I need?

One session may be sufficient, but it is more usual that one to two sessions per month are needed.

9. What risks are associated with this treatment?

Those with certain neurological disorders such as Parkinson's disease who have a deep brain stimulation device to treat their illness should refrain from receiving Sound Healing using singing bowls.

Sound Healing that uses metal singing bowls can interfere with those who have metal in their body already, such as heart pacemakers and metal implants. Also, those with certain inflammatory skin disorders may experience adverse reactions to singing bowls. For these reasons, it should be refrained from placing the bowls directly on the body.

10. Which health conditions is this energy healing practice most suitable for?

Sound Healing can be used to treat many health problems such as stress, anger, anxiety, depression, fatigue, hearing, voice and speech issues, blood and circulation problems and headaches.

Nowadays, tuning forks can be used to identify whether a bone is fractured. By striking and placing the vibrating fork close to the affected area, a diminished or absent sound would indicate a bone fracture.

Self-care tips at home

There are many ways that sound can be incorporated into your daily life.

Singing bowls are not recommended to be played by yourself unless proper training has been undertaken. This is due to the damage they can cause to hearing if played incorrectly.

I have therefore set out alternative Sound Healing methods to singing bowls.

When we are stressed, our hearing becomes blocked and restricts our energy flow.

Healing can be achieved by using the respective sounds.

Mantras

Mantras are sounds, words, syllables or phrases that can be chanted, sung or silently repeated to bring about healing.

Meditation Mantras

Meditation mantras are mantras that can be used with the breath and can be practiced twice a day for twenty minutes at a time.

The most common mantra used is SO HUM translated as "I am He/She/That." Sit comfortably with the eyes closed and breathe normally. Begin silently repeating "SO" as you inhale and "HUM" as you exhale.

Biji Mantras

Bija Mantras are one syllable sounds that can be chanted with the most popular universal mantra used being OM or AUM (pronounced ohm). OM is a deeply divine sound which vibrates at the same vibrational frequency found throughout nature and all living beings in the universe. By chanting OM, we embrace the energy of the universe.

Vocal Toning

Toning is a healing technique that involves creating elongated vowel sounds with your voice. There is no set length of time to maintain the sound. The best indication that you are doing it correctly is the ease in producing the sound. The vowel that equates to the Biji mantra, OM, is IH (pronounced 'in').

Humming Breath

Humming while exhaling helps to calm and reduce tension in the body. This exercise can be repeatedly performed for five minutes a day.

Begin by sitting upright and placing your hands around the sides of your stomach. Close your lips and keep your tongue on the roof of your mouth. Breathe in through your nose and pull air to your stomach where your hands are. Once your lungs are full, keep your lips closed and exhale while humming, making the "hmmmmmm" sound.

Guided Meditation

Guided meditation describes a type of meditation led by a teacher, either in person or via audio or video recordings. There are many guided meditation applications such as Buddhify, Calm and Headspace that you can download to your technology devices.

Listening to Music

Listening to music that uses the seven musical notes in a scale can help to heal our senses. In Indian Carnartic classical music, the notes are known as swaras. Each musical note, or swara, corresponds with each sense.

1. SMELL – Musical note C / Swara Sa
2. TASTE – Musical note D / Swara Ri
3. SIGHT – Musical note E / Swara Ga
4. TOUCH – Musical note F / Swara Ma
5. HEARING – Musical note G / Swara Pa
6. INSIGHT – Musical note A / Swara Dha
7. UNITY – Musical note B / Swara Ni

Playing Instruments

Playing musical instruments can help us to heal and each instrument corresponds to a particular sense. The instruments can also be played using the musical notes mentioned previously.

1. SMELL – Drums
2. TASTE – Trumpet
3. SIGHT – Cello
4. TOUCH – Harp
5. HEARING – Flute
6. INSIGHT – Chimes
7. UNITY – Tinkling bells

Part 5:
Implementing in Practice

The Two Stage Approach

This interactive approach can be used to restore your health and wellbeing by following two stages. The two stages factor in the energy healing practices mentioned in this book.

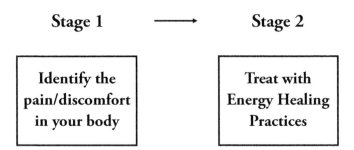

Although this approach can be used, it is always recommended that medical advice is sought from a GP regarding any health symptoms and pains you are currently experiencing.

The physical ailments in your body reveal where energy blockages exist and the areas of your body that require healing.

Stage 1: Identify Pain/Discomfort

1. **Identify Pain/Discomfort/Illness locations in the physical body with a Body Scan Meditation**

    Body scanning involves paying attention to parts of the body in a gradual sequence from the feet to the head. By mentally scanning yourself, you bring awareness to every part of your body, noticing any new and recurring aches, pain or discomfort.

Body Scan Meditation

1. Lie down or sit comfortably.
2. Breathe slowly, letting your abdomen expand and contract with each breath.
3. Bring your attention down to your feet and observe any pain and sensations that accompany it.
4. Scan your entire body, gradually moving up through your feet until you reach the top of your head. Notice any pain or discomfort.

2. Write down the pain/discomfort/illness observed from the Body Scan Meditation and rate the pain on a scale from 0 to 10

From the Body Scan Meditation, jot down all the areas where you experienced pain and set a benchmark for rating your pain. To rate the pain, circle the number on the scale below to indicate the intensity level of the pain. The scale runs from 0 – 10 with 0 equating to no pain and 10 equating to the worst pain.

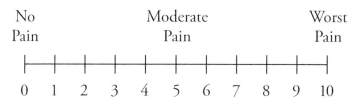

Stage 2: Heal the Pain/Discomfort

1. **Choose one energy healing practice**

   After reading about the energy healing practices, choose one healing practice that you are drawn to and feel most comfortable to try out. If you are unsure, you can make the decision on which of your senses has been distorted based on the areas of the body where you are experiencing pain or discomfort.

   If there continues to be pain in certain areas of the body then continue with the same energy healing practice that was selected at Step 1 of Stage 2 to ensure a pain free outcome is achieved. The practitioner will be able to advise how many sessions you will require to achieve the desired outcome.

   In situations when you cannot attend an energy healing practice session in person, throughout this book I have provided practical tips to self-care at home.

   It should be remembered that our energy is constantly changing since we use energy all the time. When blockages are initially noted, they can vary considerably to the next time they are checked.

2. **Repeat the Body Scan Meditation, write down the pain/discomfort/illness observed and rate the pain on a scale from 0 to 10.**

   Repeat Step 2 of Stage 1. To rate the pain, circle the number on the scale below to indicate the intensity level of the pain.

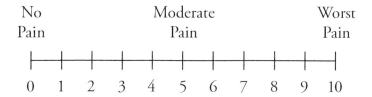

By repeating this process and rating the pain again, you will be able to compare and notice any improvements between how the pain, illness or discomfort initially felt and how it currently feels.

The aim is for the pain, illness or discomfort to disappear completely and work its way down the scale towards the rating of 0 equating to no pain.

Order for Completing the Stages

Stage 1 can be completed by the recipient prior to physically attending an energy healing practice. This will help the practitioner to concentrate on particular areas and tailor the treatment session to meet the recipient's needs.

If this is not possible, not to worry, all the stages can be completed by the practitioner during the energy healing practice itself.

Try the two stage approach yourself and record your findings. All the information you need to complete this approach can be found in this book.

On the following pages, you will find useful reference tables to help to locate the body areas affected together with a notes section where you can record observations from the body scan.

Reference Table 1
Body and Heart areas affected by Sense

	What is affected	
Sense	Areas of the Body	Emotions of the Heart
Smell	Hips, legs, lower back and male sexual organs	Anger, jealousy and aggression
Taste	Kidneys, bladder, large intestine and female sexual organs	Joy, feeling good or bad
Sight	Stomach, liver, gall bladder, pancreas and small intestine	Self-worth and confidence
Touch	Heart, lungs, circulatory system, shoulders and upper back	Love and compassion
Hearing	Throat, neck, teeth, ears and thyroid gland	Releasing feelings through expression
Insight	Eyes, face, brain, lymphatic and endocrine systems	Permission to experience feelings
Unity	Central nervous system	Cultivate bliss

Reference Table 2
Mind and Spirit areas affected by Sense

	What is affected	
Sense	Thoughts of the Mind	Lessons of the Spirit
Smell	Stability, safety and survival	Power of Freedom
Taste	Pleasure and sociability	Power of Choice
Sight	Determination, strength and personality	Power of Independence
Touch	Acceptance and sincerity	Power of Love
Hearing	Communication, inspiration and expression	Power of Will
Insight	Intuition, trust and gratitude	Power of Truth
Unity	Understanding, knowledge, spirituality	Power of Divine Connection

Readers' Notes

Readers' Notes

Part 6:
Conclusion

Conclusion

To conclude, we all have the ability to heal ourselves as energy healing uses our body's natural energy to bring about healing.

We are all made of energy. When we encounter stress and physical illness, our energy becomes blocked which reduces the amount and flow of energy within us. As a result, our senses can be distorted to reflect that energy blockages are present in our bodies. Energy healing can help us by removing these energy blockages.

Our senses resonate with particular areas of the body, emotions of the heart, thoughts of the mind and lessons of the spirit. By stimulating our senses via energy healing we can remove the energy blockages relating to all these aspects accordingly.

As energy healing stimulates our senses, it is advisable to choose an energy healing practice depending on the sense that has been distorted.

There are seven gentle energy healing practices to choose from in this book, Acupuncture, Aromatherapy, Chromotherapy, Crystal Therapy, Reflexology, Reiki and Sound Healing and for each of these, if you are unable to attend a healing treatment in person, I have suggested alternative tips how to self-care at home.

Although there are many different energy healing practices to select from, the right treatment to choose for yourself will depend on your own needs and what outcome you are seeking to achieve.

Why not try the two stage approach now to identify your pain and obtain the correct energy healing treatment you need.

Finally, thank you for taking the time to read my book and I wish you all the best for your future health and wellbeing.

Acknowledgements

I would like to take this opportunity to thank all those who helped me to write, edit and publish this book.

First, I thank God for giving me this opportunity to help others to benefit from energy healing.

I dedicate this book to my parents, Siva and Ratna Ramachandran, who have always been a great inspiration, encouragement and driving force behind all the achievements in my life. Their continued love and support behind the scenes is why you are reading this book today. Thank you for introducing me to the Divine and encouraging the spiritual side of me to prosper.

A special thanks goes to my loving husband Krishan, for helping me grow and be the best version I can be. Thank you for your love, support, time and ideas throughout this writing journey.

I would like to thank the rest of my family for their continuous support throughout the years.

Thank you to my friends for introducing me to my first energy healing session. They have also accompanied me to various energy healing seminars and treatments so that I can expand my knowledge.

Finally, I would like to thank my masters, teachers and coaches who have taught me all I know about energy healing.

About the Author

Lukshmiera Ramachandran Makwana is an intuitive energy healer and career performance coach for accountancy and tax students.

She is a certified practitioner in Reiki, Soul plan, Hypnotherapy, Coaching and Neuro Linguistic Programming (NLP). Lukshmiera also holds qualifications as a colour therapist, crystal healer, past life therapist, numerologist and tarot reader.

By profession, Lukshmiera is a Chartered Accountant and has obtained many qualifications throughout the years such as BSc (Hons), ACA (ICAEW), FCCA and ATT. She has extensive knowledge, skills and work experience in accountancy and tax which she has gained by working for leading corporate companies including one of the big four, KPMG LLP.

Printed in Great Britain
by Amazon